FINDING YOURSELF BY RENEWING YOUR MIND

Romans 12:2

MARY SHECKLES JONES

BK
ROYSTON
Publishing

BK Royston Publishing
P. O. Box 4321
Jeffersonville, IN 47131
502-802-5385
http://www.bkroystonpublishing.com
bkroystonpublishing@gmail.com

Cover Design: Gad of Elite Cover Designs
Photography Credit: LaTonya Brown

ISBN-13: 978-1-951941-17-8

Amplified Bible, Classic Edition **(AMPC)** - Copyright © 1954, 1958, 1962, 1964, 1965, 1987 by The Lockman Foundation

Darby Translation (DARBY) - Public Domain

English Standard Version Anglicised (ESVUK) - The Holy Bible, English Standard Version Copyright © 2001 by Crossway Bibles, a division of Good News Publishers.

King James Version (KJV) - Public Domain

Printed in the United States of America

DEDICATION

I am so grateful to God that He has Blessed me, strengthened me and allowed me to pour into each of you by giving me courage to write my second book.

When I wrote my first book, "From Christianity to Discipleship," I have to be honest and share that I was not ready for transparency, and thought I could skip straight to my healing and recovery. I did not want anyone to judge my journey of brokenness. But God spoke to me and told me that I missed a chapter called "Transparency." He told me that it is ok to share my testimony with others because you never know who may need to hear it.

The Bible said that we would have trials and tribulations, and Lord knows I did. But with the "Renewing of My Mind," I have found myself. Through His Love and Guidance, He never left me nor forsook me. When I was ready to come home, He was there with open arms. So, God, my Heavenly Father, this book is dedicated to you. I thank you with all of my heart and soul.

Mary

ACKNOWLEDGEMENTS

There are so many people that have contributed to making this book happen for me. First to BK Royston Publishing, (Julia Royston) who I would recommend to any author, for their professional and personal attentiveness to me. I am so pleased to be under their publishing umbrella and family.

I would like to also thank the women's group, "Women of Intent" (Vernice Mitchell). This group allowed me to "learn" to be transparent and speak my truth, and in the process share and help other women why doing so. This group allowed me a comfortable safe place to open up about your life story and not worry about being judged or frowned upon. My personal monopoly of life "Free Space." I appreciate all of you ladies and Vernice for creating this space. Thank you.

Last but not least, thanks to ALL OF MY FAMILY members. From my loving children, to my loyal siblings, and my wonderful nieces and nephews who have helped me to grow, love and prosper in many ways. From our ups, downs, the good days, bad days, and ugly days, it is all LOVE. I would not be who I am today without my family. Thank you.

And it goes without saying, thank you to my beautiful and loving parents. My Mother Mary Sheckles in Heaven watching over me, and my caring father, James Sheckles for his everlasting love, I love you both dearly and I thank you always!

In loving memory of my wonderful brother Maurice E. Stallard I.

Mary

FOREWORD

As you, the reader, study *Finding Yourself by Renewing Your Mind* by Mary Sheckles Jones, your first thought may be that she has a very good understanding of where John the Baptist and Jesus Christ were leading us as they preached, "Repent, for the Kingdom of Heaven is at hand."

The writer is saying to change your thinking, for what you are seeking is within your reach and you can have it now. Ms. Jones is expressing an idea of Mary Baker Eddy, "Thinking makes it so."

The writer is expressing an idea of Dr. Myles Munroe that finding yourself causes you to examine the purpose God has for your life when He says in Genesis 1:28: "Be fruitful, and multiply, and replenish the earth, and subdue it, and have dominion." God, who is super-consciousness guiding and directing us in the way that we should go for good health, happiness, prosperity, healing and success, wants us to change our thinking.

The readers will find that Ms. Jones is right with Isaiah 55:8 (KJV): "My thoughts are not your thoughts, neither are your ways my ways, saith the Lord."

This book can guide you in self-examination and how to see your opportunities. You will get an answer to the questions: "Does God care about me? Does He understand what I am going through? Does He know how long I have been in this situation?" This book will help you to see that God is willing to help and bless you because He needs your body in His service to make the world better than it is now.

This book will help you to see that the success, healing, prosperity, and progress you are working for and seeking are fruits of bringing your will in line with the will of your Father in heaven. He is not willing that you should perish or fail in any way. Failure is the program of the enemy of your Lord.

You can learn about the amazing grace of God that saves the lost like you and me. Grace may be the inspiration that will start you renewing your mind for the better days ahead of you.

Read and put into action every suggestion that is written for your good. Be blessed as you read *Finding Yourself by Renewing Your Mind*.

Bishop Carl Z. Liggins

TABLE OF CONTENTS

INTRODUCTION

In the book of Romans, Chapter 12:2, God is commanding us to renew our minds. Change the way we think. And not to be conformed to this world.

Renewing! Think another way! How is that? What does He mean? Why is that so?

That is so we can understand (comprehend) what He is teaching us, telling us who we are, and how to live our lives. He is saying to erase our old way of thinking, the thoughts that we have put in our minds such as, "I can't do that." That's believing in our own truth, and whatever we say about ourselves, and whatever others say or call us.

Renewing the mind is just changing the way we think and respond.

What is thinking? To begin with, it is purposeful mental activity over which we exercise some control. It is ANY mental activity that helps to formulate or solve a problem, helps make a decision, or fulfill a desire to understand. It is searching for answers and reaching for meaning. It is your MIND. This is your SOUL.

There have been many attempts to explain the nature of thinking (the MIND). We arrange words in our minds or silently whisper them within ourselves when we pray. The MIND is part of who we are, it is part of our body, part of our being, it is the BRAIN. Thinking consists more of images than of words. The MIND is also our SOUL;

this is where our emotions and our will reside as well.

We can now understand that thinking (mind) is NOT a mystical activity, unknowable, and unlearnable. This knowledge can be used to reinforce good thinking habits and to overcome bad ones.

Can thinking skills be acquired, or does one have to be born with them? It is said that good thinkers are born, not made. But teachable. The difficulty of improving our thinking depends on the habits and attitudes we have. The tasks of changing your bad habits and attitudes seems impossible, but remember that a lot of other tasks seemed so impossible at first, yet you mastered them. The unfamiliar often seems daunting or difficult to deal with. Do not be afraid of the unknown.

Romans 12:2: Jesus is asking us, commanding us not to be conformed to this world, but be transformed by the renewing of our mind. He says to change the way we used to think, and to renew our attitude, so that we may prove to ourselves what is good and acceptable to the will of God.

Verse 2 is saying that we are to discern what is the will of God. The term "the will of God" means to seek wisdom and godliness. Wisdom can be thought of as consciously applying the word of God with our renewed minds to complex moral circumstances. Godliness is how we live most of our lives, without consciously reflecting on the hundreds of things we say and do all day.

We are not to think of ourselves more highly than we ought to think, but to rate our ability with sober (calm, collected, level-headed) judgment, according to the degree of faith apportioned (given) by God to us.

Galatians 6:3 KJV: "For if a man think himself to be something when he is nothing, he deceives himself."

Romans 8:7 says to us that because the carnal mind is enmity against God, it is not subject to the law of God; neither, indeed, can it be.

1 Corinthians 2:16 is telling us to renew our minds. Who has known the mind of the Lord, that we may instruct him? Oh, but we have the mind of Christ within us.

Yes, our minds just need to be renewed, for we are made in His image.

Acts 20:19 tells us we should serve the Lord with all humility of mind, and with many tears and temptations.

I have written this book for you to understand thoroughly WHY renewing your mind is so important, and how to understand the working of the mind. God's plan is to establish and advance His Kingdom in you, by renewing your mind.

May your heart be stirred with a longing for the fulfillment of God's plan and how you will be contributing to it.

Now, put your focus on finding yourself and let God take the lead.

I want to focus on the phrase in Romans 12:2—by the renewal of your mind.

For we are perfectly useless as Christians, if we do conform to this world around us. But you can avoid all kind of worldly behaviors by just renewing your mind in Christ.

FINDING YOURSELF

Have you ever had the feeling that you were not getting everything you were supposed to get from life? A feeling that life was full of possibilities, but somehow you could never figure out how to tap into them? Somewhere in the back of your mind, a nagging feeling that there must be something more?

Many people have come to believe that life is a mystery that cannot be solved. Some even consider that life is a battle. Well, it is a battle, one that is fought within yourself.

See, life is a spiritual battle.

Life here on earth is a BATTLE.

Jesus Christ taught that it was about "GIVING and RECEIVING."

The book of Deuteronomy 28:1 (KJV) says, "If you fully obey the Lord your God and carefully follow ALL His commands, the Lord will SET YOU high above the nations on earth."

Later in the same chapter, Deuteronomy 28:15 (KJV) says, "However, if you DO NOT obey the Lord your God and do not carefully follow ALL His commands and decrees, ALL these curses will come upon you and overtake you."

This means that YOUR BLESSINGS ARE DEPENDENT UPON YOUR OBEDIENCE.

For God said in Isaiah 55:11 (KJV), "So shall my word be that goes forth out of My mouth; it shall not return to Me void, but it shall accomplish that which I please, and it shall prosper in the thing whereto I sent it. What you give is what you will receive."

To play this game of life successfully, we must train our minds by renewing them.

Romans 12:2 (KJV) says, "And be not conformed to this world, but be ye transformed by renewing of your mind, that ye may prove what is that good and acceptable and perfect will of God."

The mind plays a leading role in this game of life here on earth. Whatever you imagine in your mind, sooner or later it will materialize in your life. To train your imagination successfully, you must understand the working of your mind. You must know yourself.

The mind (brain) consists of three different levels:

1.   Subconscious—simply power, but without directions. It's like steam, it does what it wants until directed to do otherwise.

2.   Conscious—simply the carnal mind, which sees life as it is.

3.   Superconscious—the mind of God, which is in each one of us, plus the realm of perfect ideas. In it, is the perfect pattern and a perfect Divine Design for each person. In us, it is a place that we are to fill and which no one else can fill.

There is this perfect picture of this Divine Design fulfilled in the superconscious mind. It usually flashes across the conscious mind as an unattainable ideal. Something too good to be true. I have had those flashes consistently throughout my life, and I still do.

Many people are ignorant of their true destinies and are striving for things and situations that do not belong to them and would only bring failure and dissatisfaction. You need to find out who you are and who you belong to. God said it will not be easy.

When you believe you can achieve something, you will begin to direct the power of your subconscious mind to help you.

As you begin to claim your mind back from the enemy, he will not want to give up the place that he has had, and you will have to do battle with his lies and confusion.

The Bible tells us that as human beings, we are God's image-bearers, for we are made in His image, created to share in the task of bringing God's wise and truthful plan to the world.

In the book of Jeremiah 29:11 (AMP), God is telling us: "For I know the thoughts and plans that I have for you. Thoughts and plans for welfare and peace, and not for evil, to give you hope in your final outcome."

God has wonderful plans for you and me. His plan for your personal world depends on you fulfilling it by taking control of your mind (what you imagine) and your mouth (what you speak).

A person who knows the power of his words becomes very careful in his conversations. He has only to watch the impact of his words to know that his words do not go out into a void. He must recognize the power that his words can have.

Proverbs 23:7 (KJV) "For as he (man) thinketh in his heart, so is he."

What are you thinking?

That is a good question. Let me tell you about what I am thinking through this short story along with some truths.

Before I took a left turn in this walk of life, I was always thinking positive: how do I get ahead, what steps do I need to take to accomplish what I want. I was singing in the church choir, teaching Sunday School, and it was all positive thinking. Back then, my mind was centered on reaching my goals in this life while I was in the will of God. I always considered myself as walking in God's will. Until…Well, Satan is aware of our plans, especially the plans God has for you and me. And so, I woke up one morning to find myself off course.

Satan knows of God's plans before we are born. That's why God commanded that we renew our minds. The lies he (Satan) was telling me took me off my path, which led me into relationships with an array of different men. Men who seemed to have only one thing in common: DRUGS. I then voluntarily went into pleasing people instead of pleasing God. I got into the drug world in awful ways and did everything and anything that was asked of me. Realizing that it was wrong, I still felt compelled to do their bidding anyway. I went into stealing, became envious, jealous, insecure, and much more. I started lying to myself, even while I kept saying that I have to get out of this. I was lost. I had no idea of the person I had become. It took me years to realize who I was and to whom I truly belong: God.

Remember Romans 12:2 (KJV): Jesus is asking us not to be conformed to this world but be transformed by the renewing of your mind.

What got me back on the right path of looking, seeking, and finding myself for who I really am?

Isaiah 43:1 (KJV): "But now thus saith the Lord that created thee...and He that formed thee...Fear not: for I have redeemed thee, I have called thee by thy name; thou art mine."

How do we speak truth into our pain so that we can live in peace? How do we take off the old self and put on the new one?

One night while I was lying in bed next to my husband, I started crying, not knowing or really caring if he heard me or not. I pleaded and cried to the Lord: "I know that you have a better life for me than this. Hear my cry, O Lord. Help me. Please help me." While tears ran down my cheeks, my eyes started roaming around in my bedroom. My eyes were still stained from sobbing, and I was still lying next to my husband, who was still asleep. I saw a bright light standing in my bedroom door. This silhouette I saw standing there had outstretched arms. At first, I thought I was seeing things in the dark. But there He was, standing motionless, motioning to me to come to Him. I could not believe my eyes. I started feeling relaxed, calm, and at peace within myself. I silenced myself, for instantly I knew who that man was: JESUS. I said to myself, "I've been found, even though I was never along. I've been rescued." A great relief set in. I sensed a stream of powerful joy—happiness from within. I was rescued.

John 12:46 (KJV): "I am come a light into the world, that whosoever believeth on me should not abide in darkness."

For we all know that God said He will not leave us or forsake us.

In Deuteronomy 31:6, God tells us to be strong and of good courage. "Fear not, nor be terrified, for it is the Lord your God who goes with you. He will not fail you or forsake you."

Allow Jesus to rescue you from you. I did. Find yourself in Him. Don't look back; don't be like Lot's wife.

For we are significant, decision-making, world-shaping beings. This is our vocation, our purpose.

A person sooner or later will find that he is the keeper of his own soul (his own mind), the director of his life. A person with a renewed mind will imagine only good things for his life, and he will imagine every righteous desire of his heart: good health, wealth, love, friends, or just his own perfect self-expression, along with his own perfect ideas. The object of this game called life is to see clearly one's good, and to obliterate all mental pictures of evil, and to live life as an exchange of giving and receiving.

Matthew 11:28-30 (KJV): "Come unto me, all you who labor and are heavy laden, and I will give you rest. Take my yoke upon you, learn of me, for I am meek and lowly in heart, and you shall find rest unto your souls. For my yoke is easy, and my burden is light."

After seeing that silhouette, I went through a terrible illness that landed me in the hospital for a while. I had surgery that could have killed me, and I had a heart attack while on the operating table. In fact, I assume that it was just the Lord cleaning me up, that God was purifying my mind. I had an aneurysm—a blood vessel burst in my brain. He was taking out all the unrighteousness that was in my mind. It even required a section of my brain to be removed, so I would not die. I was being purged for the work unto the Lord. God had picked me up and turned me around, but God was not done. After the section of brain was removed, I had two strokes, one on a Thursday, the other that Saturday.

2 Timothy 2:21 (AMPC): "So whoever cleansed himself (from what is ignoble and unclean, who separates himself from contact with contaminating and corrupting influences) will (then himself) be a vessel set

apart and useful for honorable and noble purposes, consecrated and profitable to the Master, fit and ready for good work."

I began reading more, praising and worshipping more, even when alone. Now, I write books, telling others how I overcame by renewing my mind and trying to equip them to do the same.

While reading and writing again, I ran across this quote by Ms. Karen Ravn:

"Only as high as I reach, can I grow. Only as far as I seek, can I go. Only as deep as I look, can I see. Only as much as I dream, can I be."

Can you find yourself somewhere in that quote?

So, if you choose to find yourself, change the way you think and your usage of words. Jesus Christ taught that your words play a leading role in this game of life along with your mind. By your words you are justified, and by your words you are condemned. Many people have brought disaster into their lives through their words. You can speak life or death out of your mouth. What are you saying to yourself?

2 Timothy 2:17 (DARBY): "And their words will spread like gangrene."

Whatever you feel deeply or imagine clearly is impressed upon the subconscious mind.

The subconscious is simply power without direction, and it does what it is told to do. The subconscious mind has no sense of humor, only power, and people often joke themselves into unhappy experiences.

For example: A woman who had a great deal of money joked continually about "getting ready for the poor house." In a few years she was almost destitute; having impressed the subconscious mind with a picture of lack and limitation, she practically went there.

That thought could work both ways, it can put you in poverty and it can bring you prosperity.

You also have a conscious mind, which sees life as it is. It sees death, disaster, sickness, poverty, and limitation of every kind, and it also impress the subconscious.

What are you saying to yourself? I know if you impress the subconscious mind into finding yourself, that will be accomplished.

But we also have a superconscious mind. This is the mind of God, which is within each of us and is the realm of perfect ideas.

Jesus taught that every person has the power to bless, to heal, and to prosper. It is taught from within.

NEVER VIOLATE (overlook) A HUNCH

Matthew 7:7 (KJV): "Ask and it shall be given you, seek and ye shall find, knock and it shall be open unto you."

Jesus Christ brought out clearly that we must make the first move. He has given us our will.   How we choose to use it depends on us.

There are plenty of doors on your pathway to find yourself, but it can only be brought into manifestation through your desire, your faith, or the spoken word.

Proverb 8:35 (AMP): "For whoso finds me (Wisdom) finds life and draws forth and obtains favor from the Lord."

The object of the game of life is to see clearly your good and to obliterate all mental pictures of evil. This is only done by impressing the subconscious mind with a realization of good.

As I said before, a person who knows the power of his words becomes very careful in conversation. You only have to watch the reactions to your words to know that words do what they were sent to do. Your words could hurt people, belittle them, take away self-esteem, or they could motivate people, encourage them, and grow them. What are you saying when you speak to yourself or others? I say bridle your tongue and call on the law of forgiveness—which is God's law. For God has the power to forgive or neutralize your mistakes.

I know, in my own case, it took me a long while to come out of a belief that I knew would only bring disappointment. I found the only way I could make a change in my life was to change my subconscious mind, change the way others were speaking to me, seeing me. I started speaking with confidence and forcefully within myself, "For I am the Kingdom of Heaven, for I am the RIGHTEOUSNESS of God, that is what is in me." There is only one power—God's power. There are no disappointments in Him, and that means a happy life. I noticed a change gradually, then happiness commenced coming my way. Change your mind, change your life. I faced this situation fearlessly until there was no situation to face at all. It all fell away on its own, for I had renewed my mind.

If you are afraid to change, you are giving into a belief of good and evil, instead of one. God is absolute; there can be no opposing power, unless you make the falseness of evil for yourself.

Someone once said that courage contains genius and magic. Rub the lantern, find the true you, the only you. Allow this genie to show you what you will see. Believe in only one power—God's power.

Now, walk under the ladder of life. It's impossible to see because of your thoughts that are holding you back. It could be a big moment in your life if this ladder didn't hold you in bondage. If you are willing to do something that you are afraid to do, you will set yourself free. You will be able to find yourself. What a man says of others will be said of him, and what he wishes for another, he is wishing for himself. Life is about giving and receiving. Sometimes facing the unknown can deter you from being or doing what God had given you to do.

Take me for example. I had made plans to move to Texas, but doubt started flowing in my mind. "Are you sure starting over is what you want to do? People are beginning to know who you are here, your name is getting to the right people, etc." Then, I started talking to God, and it became clear about the feelings of doubt that I was having. He told me that what I was feeling was not doubt, it was fear of starting over, it was fear of the unknown. He said, "DON'T BE AFRAID, FOR YOU ARE NEVER ALONE, FOR I AM WITH YOU WHEREVER YOU ARE." His presence is always with you, too. So, if you have those feelings of doubt, break that chain and move forward. God does have a plan for you.

When you believe, you will succeed or have what you want. It's only a matter of time. Your belief, your direct instruction, will direct your subconscious mind. Now, this is power in believing. Your subconscious mind always responds to your beliefs and creates what you believe. So, you will have to fill your mind with positive beliefs about being able to achieve your goal, which is to find yourself. So, take a look at what you believe. Whatever you are imagining, begin changing or enforcing those beliefs, so that you send the right message to the subconscious mind, and make sure that you create the right situations you want to send out. When you believe you can achieve something, you will begin to direct the power of your subconscious mind to help you succeed so that you achieve the outcome you want. So, start changing those beliefs and you will begin directing the subconscious mind to create more of what you want.

To create new beliefs, first you should start changing your thoughts—because thoughts lead to beliefs. What you think about all the time you will eventually believe. You will also have to change the way you see things, because what you see is what you believe. That is your carnal mind (your conscious) at work. This also means changing the way you see yourself. Because how you see yourself is what you believe. To properly work with mind power and to direct your subconscious mind, you need to have a belief that is in line with what you want to achieve, because what you believe is what you get.

Your beliefs should help you succeed, not hold you back. If you have a belief that says, "You can do this," then that belief will allow you to succeed to find yourself. That belief is what the subconscious mind will pick up, and the power of your subconscious will make it possible for you to do what you have set out to do.

As indicated in my earlier discussion of the three different departments of the brain, the power that is in your subconscious mind will be directed to your superconscious mind (the mind of God). That power will change your thoughts as well.

What is needed is a new set of keys to unlock all that God is holding for you. Keys that will help you to escape those "PRISONS OF THE MIND." You must realize that the Word of God has the power to realign anything that is misaligned. You do not have to continue mindlessly walking in the dark for the right path through life. God already has your success all planned out.

Man can change his conditions by changing his words.

Proverbs 18:2 (KJV): "Death and life are in the power of the tongue."

The transformation of our mind is the work of the Holy Spirit. What does the Spirit do to transform us into the image of God? He enables us to "behold the glory of the Lord." This is how the mind is renewed—by gazing at the glories of Christ for what they really are. But to enable us to do that, the Spirit has work to do. He must work in both directions: from the outside in and from the inside out. Working from the outside in by exposing the mind of Christ is exalting truth. He must lead us to hear the gospel, to read the Bible, to study Christ-exalting writings of great spiritual teachers, and to meditate on the perfections of Christ.

This is exactly what our enemy does not want us to do. In 2 Corinthians 4:4(ESVUK)—"The god of this world (Satan) has blinded the minds of the unbelievers, to keep them from seeing the light of the gospel of the glory of Christ, who is the image of God." Because to see that for what it really is will renew the mind and transform the life and produce unending worship.

The Holy Spirit's work from the inside out is breaking the hard heart that binds and corrupts the mind. The purpose of breaking the hard heart is so the truth would not be despised and rejected. And if he only humbled the hard heart, but put no Christ-exalting truth before the mind, there would be no Christ to embrace, and no worship would happen.

Reflection

_____

_____

_____

_____

_____

_____

_____

_____

_____

_____

_____

_____

_____

_____

_____

_____

WHO ARE YOU IN CHRIST?

We will never have a proper understanding of who we are until we know who God is. The knowledge of God and the knowledge of self always go hand in hand. There can be no true knowledge of self apart from the knowledge of God. He is the only reference point.

In the book of Hebrews 5:12 (KJV), God is saying that in fact, though by this time you ought to be teachers, you need someone to teach you the elementary truths of God's word all over again. You need milk, not solid food.

In Isaiah 40:29-31 (KJV), God says that He giveth power to the faint; and to them that have no might he increase strength, even the youths shall faint and be weary, and the young shall utterly fall. But they that wait upon the Lord shall renew their strength; they shall mount up with wings as eagles; they shall run, and not be weary; and they shall walk, and not faint.

God cares how you feel about your life. The first thing you need to know is that God has feelings. I can give you a lot of Scriptures on this, but I will give you one:

Hebrews 4:15 (AMPC): "For we have not a High Priest who is unable to understand and sympathize and have a shared feeling with our weaknesses and infirmities and liability to the assaults of temptation, but One who has been tempted in every aspect as we are, yet without sinning."

The Bible is all about the feelings of God.

In the book of Mark 8:27-30 (KJV), Jesus was having a conversation with His disciples regarding identity.

He asked, "WHO DO PEOPLE SAY I AM?" The disciples responded with who others thought He was. So, he asked again, "WHO DO YOU SAY I AM?"

"Thou art the Christ!!!"

Now, I ask you: Who do you say you are? Who do you say Jesus is?

If you live in an aimless and defeated manner with no confidence, it seeps into every area of your life—your health, mental well-being, emotional stability, and spiritual strength.

Who do I say I am? I am a follower of Christ, yet I am a wounded warrior. I used to be that girl who was lost and had no identity. I was fearful and struggled with my own identity. I knew God loved me, and I knew He wanted me to live in victory. So, I kept telling myself that, in Romans 8:1, God was telling me that there was no condemnation for those who are in Christ Jesus, because through Christ Jesus, the law of the Spirit of life has set me free from the law of sin and death.

Jesus is more than a good man. He is God revealed in flesh. He came to rescue you and me from eternal sin and death. He died for our sins and rose in victory. Knowing who you are starts with knowing who He is.

Learn to know Jesus, as He is, for yourself. Others may see Jesus as a judge, but He is the opposite. He is a loving God of mercy and grace. He is slow to anger and will not hold your faults against you. His plans for your life are to prosper, not to harm you. He is good and His loving kindness endures forever.

Knowing who you are originates in knowing who He is.

When you know who you are in Christ, you will change the world.

Identity is found when you know who you are in Christ, who He is and how He loves us. For we are His children. Understanding how valued you are and how righteous He has made you, contributes to who you are in Him. Once you know how accepted and free He has made you, you can't help but become steadfast in your true self—a Christian.

When you know who you are in Christ, you will change the world. Once you understand who you truly are in Christ, you will go from ordinary to Christian superpower. By surrendering your will to God's will, you fulfill the prophecy of Jesus.

When we come to God, He gives us a new identity. He says that we become His children, and we have access to all His resources of power. Yet, we so often continue to see ourselves in our old ways.

In order to learn the ways of Jesus, you first need to understand how God sees you! You need to understand who you really are!

When you said "yes" to God, you stepped into a new identity. But, just knowing will not make the difference until you begin to walk it. When you begin to understand ALL that your new identity means, you can begin to live in the truth of who God says you are, rather than in the way you have come to see yourself through the ups and downs life has brought your way.

You are God's treasured child—you do not get your identity from what you have done, or from what has been done to you. You do not get your identity from what other people have said to you or about you. You get your identity from what God says about you. He's your father, He created you to be all He knows you can be. Plus, He is like NO earthly Father. Put away the mentality of the past and step into who you are because of Jesus.

Just know this for certain:

1.   You are loved. (John 3:16)

2.   You are called Jesus' friend. (John 15:15)

3.   You are forgiven. (Colossians 1:14)

4.   You are God's adopted child. (Ephesians 1:5)

5.   You can be sure, that because God started a good work in your heart, He will complete it. (Philippians 1:6)

6.   You have a future and a hope. He has plans for you. (Jeremiah 29:11)

Absorb the truth of who you are in God's sight. When thoughts of low self-esteem and insecurity take over your mind, learn how to take those thoughts captive and replace them with the truth of what God says about you.

Say this short prayer when feeling low.

Father God, thank you for telling me and assuring me that I am precious and significant in your sight! Help me today to believe it and to walk in my new identity! In Jesus' mighty name. Amen

Here is a list of more Scriptures that will tell you who you are:

1.   I am greatly loved by God. (Ephesians 2:4)

2. I am renewed in the knowledge of God and no longer want to live in my old ways or nature before I accepted Christ. (Colossians 3:9-10)

3. I am chosen by God who called me out of darkness of sin and into the light and life of Christ so I can proclaim the excellence and greatness of who He is. (1 Peter 2:9)

4. I am born again—spiritually transformed, renewed, and set apart for God's purpose—through the living and everlasting Word of God. (1 Peter 1:23)

5. I overcome the enemy of my soul by the blood of the lamb and the word of my testimony. (Revelation 12:11)

6. I am free from the law of sin and death. (Romans 8:2)

7.   I have received the Spirit of Wisdom and revelation in the knowledge of Jesus, the eyes of my heart enlightened, so that I know the hope of having life in Christ. (Ephesians 1:17-18)

8.   The Spirit of God, who is greater than the enemy in the world, lives in me. (1 John 4:4)

The book of Deuteronomy 14:2 (KJV) states, "For thou art a holy people unto the Lord thy God, and the Lord hath chosen thee to be a peculiar people unto himself, above all the nations."

1 Peter 2:9 (KJV) states, "But you are a chosen people, a royal priesthood, a holy nation, a people belonging to God, that you may declare the praises of Him who called

you out of darkness into His wonderful light."

God is saying be holy, and set yourself apart, for He is holy.

But 1 Peter 2:11 (NIV) says: "Dear friends, I urge you, as aliens and strangers in the world, to abstain from sinful desires, which is war against your souls (brain). Live such good lives (prosper) among the pagans that, though they accuse you of doing wrong, they may see your good deeds and glorify God on the day He visits us."

Paul is telling us to prepare (renew) our minds for action. Be self-controlled and set our hope fully on the grace to be given.

OBEDIENCE: GOD'S WILL IN ACTION

Obedience is faith in action. Obedience stems from being spiritually focused with a purpose. Seeking the purpose of God is not an easy road to travel. But if we stay committed, then we will see great results in the end. Wavering back and forth, in and out of God's will, is going to extend frustration and time in the wilderness.

Choose to do one thing: THE WILL OF GOD.

READ ROMANS 12: 1-2

QUESTION 1 - How committed will you be in pursing the will of God?

_____

_____

_____

_____

QUESTION 2 - CONVERSATION WITH GOD PSALM 143:10

What is God saying to you through this scripture?

_____

_____

_____

_____

What do I want to tell God in response to what He is saying?

_____

_____

_____

_____

RENEWING THE MIND DESTRUCTIVE THOUGHT PATTERNS

Write down any destructive or unhealthy though patterns you have in regard to:

Yourself—appearance, worth, life situation

Others—appearance, worth, life situation

God—who He is, how He views you, His role in your life

_____

_____

_____

_____

_____

_____

_____

_____

Reflection

_____

_____

_____

_____

_____

_____

_____

_____

_____

_____

_____

_____

_____

_____

_____

_____

_____

_____

_____

_____

_____

IDENTIFY THE LIES

Upon what lies are your thoughts based? Ask yourself, "When do I typically have these thoughts? In what situations do these thoughts occur?"

_____

_____

_____

_____

_____

_____

_____

_____

_____

_____

_____

_____

_____

_____

Reflection

_____

_____

_____

_____

_____

_____

_____

_____

_____

_____

_____

_____

_____

_____

_____

_____

_____

_____

_____

THE IMPORTANCE OF RENEWING YOUR MIND

I can recall when I first learned about the phrase, "Change your thoughts, and you will change your life." That means that if you really want things to become different, you have to change the way you are thinking and seeing yourself. I learned this and much more about why it was important to renew my mind from my reading and research years ago before I took a wrong turn in my life. But, even knowing what I knew, I still needed to renew my mind to help myself. So, that became very important to me. I started working on myself, started speaking positively to myself, and seeing myself in a different view. I started having those flashes of Divine Design from my super-conscious again. I began by seeking what was important by renewing my mind, and I soon saw that my old way of thinking had become a habit, a challenge that I had to conquer.

To better understand the concept of renewing the mind, first you have to understand that it is God's perfect will for all people to be saved and to come into the knowledge of the truth. Second, you need to know that God reveals His will for mankind through His Word.

As you study and put God's Word into practice, you will come to understand God's Will for your life by renewing your mind. Jesus and God's Will are one.

John 1:14 says, "In the beginning the Word already existed. So, the Word became human and made His home among us. He was full of unfailing love and faithfulness, and we have heard of His glory!" The Bible is God's testimony of what He has already prepared for His children. It is the Father's will for His family to know His thought and live our lives His way so that we can enjoy all that Jesus has to offer. The Bible is God speaking to us now. God's Word is alive. Be careful how you speak to others. You can fearlessly act on the written Word of God, by renewing your mind, just as you would if Jesus had called your name and spoken with you personally.

Renewing your mind requires faith, and faith is acting on the Word of God. You speak the Word in order to change the way you think about your life, your work, your everything. Through His written Word, God has provided the way for you to renew your mind, to change the way you think. The Word allows you to know Him and approach your life in a way that pleases Him.

The renewing of your mind will bring your will into agreement with the Father's will. You will want to fill your mind with the Word of God. When difficulties or decisions arise, you will automatically see how important it is to see them through the eyes of God's Word.

The Father desires that His children be free and live victoriously over the evil caused by Satan. He wishes for you to live His Word because it is the key to your deliverance and success. This is one importance of renewing your mind.

The Bible is full of reasons why it is important to renew your mind. Remember, when you do become a child of God, your identity will change as well.

In Jeremiah 1:5, God is telling us that He knew us before we were born. And He is also saying that we were sanctified and ordained a prophet unto the nations. If you don't renew your mind, this is something that you will never know.

The book of Luke 12:7-12 lets us know that God even knows the number of hairs on our head.

By renewing your mind, you will receive the grace and spiritual peace that

God has given His children. This too is an important reason to renew your mind. This grace that God is offering is His unmerited favor, something that we don't even deserve. He has even adopted us as His own, meaning He chooses us because it pleases Him, for we were destined, and He was very kind to us, which He did freely. We were even redeemed through His blood. He even forgave our sins, shortcomings, and trespasses according to His riches and the generosity of His grace. He gave us every kind of wisdom and understanding (practical insight and prudence) and made known to us the mystery of His Will (his plans and purpose). All this will be revealed once we renew our minds. Ephesians 1:11-12 (KJV) says, "In whom also we have obtained an inheritance, being predestined according to the purpose of Him who worketh all things after the counsel of His own will, that we should be to the praise of his glory, who were first in Christ."

All this we need to know if we are to renew our mind in Christ. Plus, this is very important.

In Hebrews 5:12-14 (KJV), God is also saying that we need to renew our mind. "For when the time ye ought to be teachers, ye have need that one teach you again which be the first principles of the oracles of God; and are become such as have need of milk, and not of strong meat. For everyone that uses milk is unskillful in the word of righteousness; for he is a babe. But, strong meat belongs to them that are of full age, even those by reason of use, have had their senses exercised by discerning both good and evil."

Learn from God, about God. Renewing your mind is a fresh start in knowing who you are. Now, that is very important.

John 3:3 (KJV) tells us that unless a person be born again, he cannot see the kingdom of God.

The Christian alternative to immoral behavior and attitudes is not a new list of moral behaviors or attitudes. It is the triumphant power and transformation of the Holy Spirit through faith in Jesus Christ, our Savior, our Lord.

God has made us sufficient to be ministers in His new covenant, not of the letter but of the Spirit. So, transformation is a profound, blood-bought change from the inside out. Renewed Mind.

In Romans 12:2 (KJV), "the renewal of the mind" is form of transformation within yourself. This is very crucial and very important.

a.   If you long to break loose from conformity to the world, renew your mind.

b.   If you long to be transformed and new from the inside out.

c.   If you long to be free from mere duty-driven Christianity and do what you love to do because what you love to do is what you ought to do.

d.   If you long to offer up your body as a living sacrifice so that your whole life becomes a spiritual act of worship and displays the worth of Christ above the worth of the world.

Then give yourself, with all of your might, to pursuing this—the renewal of your mind. Because the Bible says, this is the key to beginning your transformation.

The mind has a "spirit." In other words, our mind has what we call a "mindset." It doesn't just have a view, it has a viewpoint. It doesn't just have the power to perceive and detect. It also has a posture (behaving in a way that is intended to impress or mislead), a demeanor (outward behavior), a bearing (the way one stands or moves), an attitude (a way of thinking or feeling about someone or something, reflected in a person's behavior), a bent (dishonest, corrupt, etc.). "Be renewed in the spirit of your mind." It has a spirit, a mindset that is hostile to the supremacy of God. Remember, our minds are bent on not seeing God as infinitely more worthy of praise than we are, or the things we make or achieve.

The Bible says we have exchanged the glory of the immortal God for images resembling mortal man. An image in the mirror is the mortal image we worship most. That's what's wrong with our minds. This is the relationship between verses 1 and 2 of Romans 12. Verse 1 says that we should present our bodies as a living sacrifice which is our spiritual service of worship. So, the aim of our life is worship. We are to use our bodies to display the worth of God and all that he is for us in Christ. So, doesn't it make perfect sense when verse 2 says that our minds must be renewed? Because our minds are not by nature God-worshipping minds. They are by nature self-worshipping minds. That is the spirit of our minds.

You must no longer walk as the others do, in the futility of their minds. They are darkened in their understanding, alienated from the life of God because of the ignorance that is in them, due to their hardness of heart. Our mental suppression of liberating truth is rooted in our hardness of heart. Our hard hearts will not submit to the supremacy of Christ, and therefore our blind minds cannot see the supremacy of Christ.

There is a kind of knowledge of God that transforms us because it liberates us from the deceit and the power of our fleshly desires.

The word "renewal." It is the Holy Spirit. The Holy Spirit renews the mind.

It is very important to renew your mind, for the knowledge of God awaits you.

Read your Bible from cover to cover, always in search of the revelation of the glory of Christ. Read and meditate on the words that you read. And pray that the Holy Spirit will renew your mind, that you may desire and approve the will of God, so that all of life will become worship to the glory of Christ.

A little something that I found in a hymn and the lyrics are by Katie Barclay Wilkinson (1859-1928)

Music by: A. Cyril Gould (Public Domain)

May the mind of Christ, my Savior, live in
me from day to day,
By His love and power controlling all I do
and say,

May the Word of God dwell richly in my
heart from hour to hour,
so that all may see I triumph only through
his pow'r.

After renewing your mind, you may wish to rededicate your life back to Christ.

Some questions you may want to ask yourself:

1.   Have I lost my relationship with God because of sin?   (NO)

        a.   Luke 15: 11-24

        b.   Ephesians 1:7

        c.   Romans 5:20

2.   How will the Father view my past sins?

        a.   Isaiah 1: 18

        b.   Isaiah 43:25

        c.   Hebrews 8:12

        d.   Psalm 103:12

3.   What do I do about my sin?

        a.   1 John 1:9

        b.   1 John 2:1-2

c.   Proverbs 28:13

d.   Philippians 3:12-14

.

www.ingramcontent.com/pod-product-compliance
Lightning Source LLC
Chambersburg PA
CBHW051700090426
42736CB00013B/2470